Giraffes

and Other Hoofed Mammals

Concept and Product Development: Editorial Options, Inc.
Series Designer: Karen Donica
Book Author: Meish Goldish

For information on other World Book
products, visit us at our Web site at
http://www.worldbook.com

For information on sales to schools and libraries
in the United States, call 1-800-975-3250.

For information on sales to schools and libraries
in Canada, call 1-800-837-5365.

World Book, Inc.
233 N. Michigan Ave.
Chicago, IL 60601

Library of Congress Cataloging-in-Publication Data

Giraffes and other hoofed mammals.
       p. cm. -- (World Book's animals of the world)
    ISBN 0-7166-1213-5 -- ISBN 0-7166-1211-9 (set)
    1. Giraffe--Juvenile literature. 2. Ungulates--juvenile literature. [1. Giraffe.
    2. Ungulates.] I. World Book, Inc. II. Series.

    QL737.U56 G57 2001
    599.638--dc21

                                                                              2001017522

Printed in Singapore

1 2 3 4 5 6 7 8 9 05 04 03 02 01

World Book's Animals of the World

Giraffes
and Other Hoofed Mammals

What does it take to get a drink of water around here?

World Book, Inc.
A Scott Fetzer Company
Chicago

Contents

What's special about my stripes?

Just who else has horns like these?

What's my tongue doing up in a tree?

What Is a Hoofed Mammal?

A hoofed mammal is one that has hoofs. A hoof is the hard covering on a mammal's foot. It is made of a hard substance called horn. A hoof is like a thick, tough toenail around the foot. Hoofs help a mammal walk and run on its toes.

Hoofed mammals are called ungulates *(UHNG gyuh lihts).* Ungulates are alike in certain ways. Most ungulates, like the giraffe you see here, are even-toed. They have two or four toes on each foot. Some ungulates, like the zebra, are odd-toed. They have one or three toes on each foot.

Giraffe hoof   Zebra hoof

Giraffe

Where in the World Do Giraffes Live?

Hoofed mammals are found in many parts of the world. But giraffes live only in Africa. They are found south of the Sahara *(suh HAIR uh)*. They live in open grasslands with scattered trees and shrubs. For safety, giraffes usually stay away from thick forests. The many trees there can slow them down if they have to run quickly from a lion.

There is only one species, or kind, of giraffe. But not all giraffes are the same. There are eight different groups of giraffes. Each group of giraffes has a different coat pattern. The pattern is a clue to which group a giraffe belongs to.

Different groups of giraffes live in different parts of Africa. For example, Masai *(muh SY)* giraffes live in eastern Africa. Nigerian *(ny JIHR ee uhn)* giraffes live in central and western Africa. Transvaal *(tranz VAHL)* giraffes live in southern Africa.

World Map

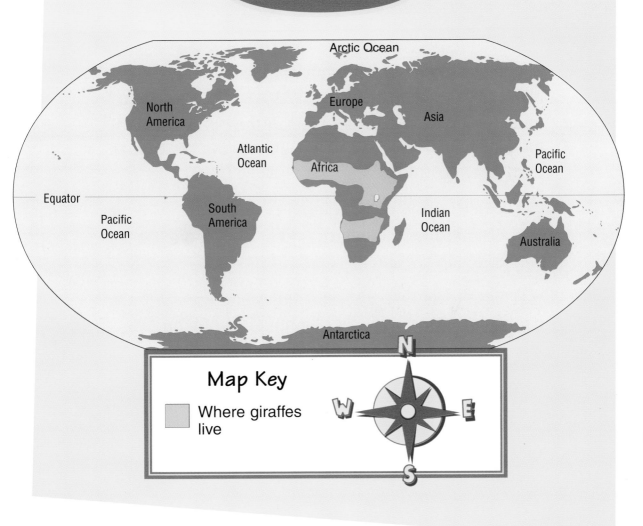

Arctic Ocean

North America

Europe

Asia

Atlantic Ocean

Africa

Pacific Ocean

Equator

Pacific Ocean

South America

Indian Ocean

Australia

Antarctica

Map Key

Where giraffes live

How Do Hoofs Help a Giraffe?

Hoofs help a giraffe in many ways. First, they allow the animal to run quickly. Sometimes a giraffe must run from an attacking lion. If the giraffe had flat feet, it couldn't move so fast. But a giraffe on its toes can really go!

Second, hoofs help a giraffe defend itself. A giraffe can kick hard with its sharp hoofs. One strong blow can kill a lion.

Third, hoofs help a giraffe stand and walk. A baby giraffe can stand up within an hour after being born—thanks to those hoofs!

Giraffe running

How Close Are a Baby Giraffe and Its Mother?

Like all mammals, giraffes give birth to live young. A baby giraffe is called a calf. After a calf is born, it stays close to its mother. The calf depends on its mother for food and protection. A calf drinks its mother's milk for 9 or 10 months. It also starts to eat green plants at the age of 2 weeks.

A calf may stand about 6 feet (1.8 meters) tall at birth. That is about as tall as an adult man. The calf weighs about 150 pounds (68 kilograms).

A giraffe is one of the few animals born with horns. Most other hoofed mammals with horns grow their horns when they are older. Giraffe horns start as small, bony lumps covered with skin and hair. The lumps grow longer as the calf grows bigger.

A calf grows quickly. In its first year, it may grow about 1 inch (2.5 centimeters) a week. By its first birthday, the giraffe may already stand 10 feet (3 meters) tall!

Giraffe mother and calf

Why Do Baby Giraffes Need Baby Sitters?

Baby giraffes stay close to their mothers for about a year. But part of each day, the mothers must go off to find food for themselves. The calves stay behind in a group. One adult female giraffe watches over the group. She may even give milk to a calf that is hungry.

Young giraffes are not allowed to go off on their own to look for food. That would be too dangerous. Calves have many enemies that wait to attack them. Their enemies include lions, leopards, cheetahs, hyenas, and crocodiles. The calves are much safer with their baby sitter watching over them!

Calves with baby sitter

How Tall Can a Giraffe Get?

Giraffes are the world's tallest animals. An adult male grows about 17 feet (5.2 meters) high. That's almost as tall as three grown men standing on each other's shoulders! A female giraffe grows about 14 feet (4.3 meters) high.

Female giraffes reach their full size by about age 5. Males are fully grown by about age 8. By then, everything about a giraffe is big! Its legs are 6 feet (1.8 meters) long. So is its neck. An adult male giraffe weighs about 2,600 pounds (1,800 kilograms).

A giraffe's tail is about as long as a yardstick—3 feet (91 centimeters)! Add the hairs at the end of the tail, and the length doubles. A giraffe's tongue is about 21 inches (53 centimeters) long. Use a yardstick or ruler to see how long that is!

Adult giraffe

What's Inside a Giraffe's Neck?

Inside a giraffe's neck are seven bones. These bones and a giraffe's backbone are its vertebrae *(VUR tuh bree).* Most other mammals, including humans, also have seven neck bones. But a giraffe's neck bones are much longer. Each bone is about 10 inches (25 centimeters) long.

A giraffe's neck also holds a windpipe. The windpipe carries air from the animal's nose and mouth to its lungs. A giraffe's lungs are extra large. They pump air through the long neck.

A giraffe's neck muscles are very strong. They support the long, heavy neck bones. When a giraffe lifts its head and neck, it is lifting about 550 pounds (250 kilograms).

Giraffes use their necks in many ways. They use them to reach tall tree leaves to eat. Two fighting giraffes push their necks against each other.

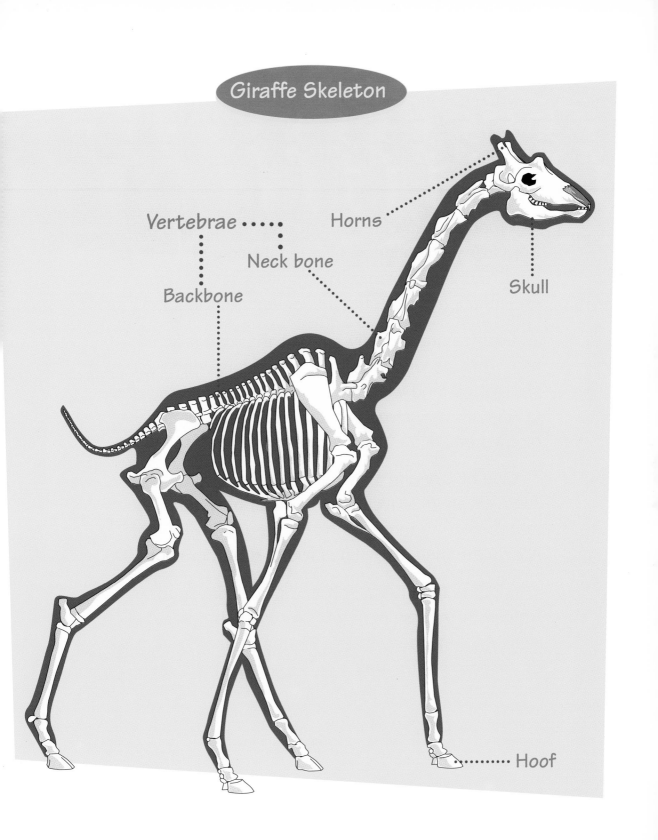

Giraffe Skeleton

Vertebrae ·····

Horns

Neck bone

Skull

Backbone

Hoof

How Does a Giraffe Browse?

When a giraffe browses, it eats leaves and buds from trees and bushes. Like most hoofed mammals, giraffes only eat plants. The giraffe uses its upper lip and long tongue to strip the leaves from the tree.

Giraffes are the only animals that can reach the high treetops without climbing. Giraffes don't have to share their food with other creatures while browsing. In Africa, many trees end up with flat tops after giraffes eat all their top leaves and branches.

One of a giraffe's favorite foods is acacia (uh KAY shuh) leaves. Acacia trees have very sharp thorns. But the thorns don't hurt a giraffe as it eats. A giraffe's thick, hairy lips protect it as it browses.

Giraffes tend to eat, off and on, all day long. At first, they chew their food very little before swallowing it. Later, they bring the cud, or food, back up to their mouths and chew it again. This makes the food easier to digest.

Giraffe browsing

How Does a Giraffe Drink Water?

A giraffe's neck is long enough to reach a high treetop. Yet it is too short to reach the ground. That makes it hard for a giraffe to bend down for water. To get a drink, a giraffe must first spread its front legs wide apart. Then it lowers its head to the water.

A giraffe drinks for a few seconds at a time. After five or six drinks, the giraffe is full. These drinks may add up to more than 10 gallons (37.9 liters) of water!

Giraffes are very cautious at waterholes. While bending down to drink, giraffes cannot see enemies that can be coming up on them from behind. Often, giraffes go to a waterhole in a group. Several giraffes stay on guard while the others drink.

Giraffes can go several days without drinking water. That's because the acacia leaves they eat are very moist. Also, giraffes try to conserve their energy. So they don't often feel thirsty.

Giraffe drinking

Why Do Giraffes Travel in Herds?

Giraffes travel in groups, or herds, to protect themselves from enemies. A lion may attack a giraffe that is by itself. But the lion is less likely to attack a giraffe in a herd. There's safety in numbers!

The size of a giraffe herd often changes. A giraffe may leave the herd to be by itself. Or it may leave one herd to join another. At any time, a herd may have 50 or more giraffes. Or it may have as few as 3 or 4.

Male giraffes often roam the grasslands by themselves. Females usually stay in pairs or small groups. A male will join the female herd when a member of the herd is ready to mate.

Giraffe herd

Why Does a Giraffe Rock When It Walks?

A giraffe walks differently from most other four-legged animals. First it moves both feet on one side of its body. Then it moves both feet on the other side. This causes the giraffe to rock from side to side as it walks. Get down on your hands and knees and try to move that way. It feels weird, right?

Giraffes may rock, but they do just fine as runners. A giraffe can gallop up to 35 miles (56.5 kilometers) an hour. Just don't expect it to move that fast for long. Giraffes tire very easily. In general, they would much rather walk than run.

Giraffe walking

How Does a Giraffe Sleep?

Getting into a comfortable position for sleep is not easy for a giraffe. That's why a giraffe often sleeps standing up. It simply lowers its neck and tail and lets its eyelids droop.

Sometimes a giraffe will bend its legs and lie down to sleep. It holds its neck up straight, or it rests it on its hip or on a tree branch. When a herd lies down, one member always stays awake to watch.

No matter how they rest, giraffes get very little real sleep. At night, they usually fall into a deep sleep for only three to five minutes at a time. They enjoy about five deep sleeps a night.

Giraffe resting

Are Giraffes Good Company?

Many African animals find giraffes to be good company. Since giraffes are so tall, they are excellent "lookout towers." They can spot danger long before other animals. Sometimes, giraffes in a herd will suddenly turn their heads to stare in one direction. That tells other animals that danger may lie ahead.

Giraffes are usually very calm and gentle. They do not hunt or chase after other animals. They do not like to fight. They would rather run away than fight. But giraffes will defend themselves if a lion attacks them.

One of the giraffe's best friends is the tiny tickbird. Tickbirds ride on the giraffe's body. They eat ticks and other insects off the giraffe's coat. The bird helps the giraffe keep clean. At the same time, the giraffe's ticks make a good meal for the birds. What a perfect friendship!

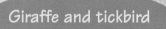
Giraffe and tickbird

What Is Special About a Giraffe's Coat?

All mammals have fur or hair on their bodies. Giraffes are no exception. But a giraffe's coat is special because it is like a fingerprint. Each giraffe has its own distinct pattern.

Different groups of giraffes have coats of different colors and designs. Three different kinds of giraffes are shown in this photo, which was taken on a wildlife preserve. The Reticulated *(rih TIHK yuh LAY tuhd)* giraffe, on the left, has large tan spots that are separated by thin white lines. The Southern giraffe, in the middle, has lighter spots. The Rothschild's giraffe, on the right, has dark spots with leafy edges.

Even within the same group of giraffes, no two coats are identical. A baby giraffe can recognize its mother by her unique coat pattern.

Three kinds of giraffes

Who Is the Giraffe's Closest Relative?

Only one animal is closely related to the giraffe. It is the okapi *(oh KAH pee).* It is a rare animal that lives near the Congo River in Africa.

Like the giraffe, the male okapi has two small horns on its head. A female okapi does not grow horns. An okapi's body slopes downward like a giraffe's. And the okapi has a long black tongue to strip leaves off trees. It also uses its tongue to wash its own eyes!

Strangely, the okapi hardly looks like a giraffe. In fact, it looks more like a horse or a zebra. The okapi stands about 5 feet (1.5 meters) tall. Its neck is much shorter than a giraffe's. And its legs have stripes like a zebra's.

Okapi

Who Grows Antlers Instead of Horns?

Many hoofed mammals, like the giraffe and okapi, grow horns. But elk and other deer are the only mammals that grow antlers. Antlers are not the same as horns. Antlers are temporary. They shed, but they grow back each year. Horns are permanent. They stay with an animal its whole life.

Antlers are covered by a soft, velvetlike layer. When the covering dies, the deer rub it off. Horns are covered by skin. The covering makes the horns very hard and tough.

Its antlers help this elk stay cool. Warm blood rushes to its antlers. The outside air cools the blood. As a result, the animal's whole body cools off. That's a pretty cool fact!

Antlers are much larger than horns, too. Antlers sometimes look like tree branches. Their sharp points warn predators to stay away.

Elk

Whose Hoofprint Looks Like a Heart?

The hoofprint of a white-tailed deer is shaped like a heart. The deer's hoof is cloven *(KLOH vuhn),* or divided. Each foot has two large, curved toes. The curves leave a heart-shaped print in the dirt when the deer walks.

Hoofprint of a white-tailed deer

Deer use their hoofs for running quickly. But they also use them to signal danger. When a female senses trouble, she stomps her hoof hard on the ground. This tells other deer in the herd to run away.

Deer can run extremely fast. Their legs are long, thin, and light in weight. Running on their hoofs gives deer extra speed and bounce. Deer can usually outrun their enemies. A white-tailed deer can run up to 40 miles (64 kilometers) an hour. It can leap up to 20 feet (6.1 meters) in a single jump.

White-tailed deer

How Are a Caribou's Hoofs Like Snowshoes?

A caribou *(KAR uh boo)* is a kind of large deer. It travels a lot on deep snow. You might think that its feet would sink hard into the snow with each step it takes. But that does not happen. A caribou's hoof is split and spread wide apart. Its shape works like a snowshoe to keep the caribou on top of the snow.

A caribou's hoofs are well protected. Long hair grows down over the hoofs and covers them. A caribou also has a special gland that gives off a greasy material. This material helps protect the hair around the hoof from snow and ice. Above each hoof are two long toes called dewclaws. They give a caribou extra support when it walks in snow.

Every spring, large herds of caribou migrate to the Arctic tundra for food. The caribou walk hundreds of miles on ice and snow. They use their hoofs to dig for food. Their feet are tough!

Caribou

When Do Moose Go Swimming?

Moose live near water. Like most other hoofed mammals, they are herbivores *(HUR buh vawrz),* or plant-eaters. In the summer, they like to eat plants that grow by rivers and lakes. Moose stick their heads into the water to get food. Sometimes they dive into the water and swim to the bottom to reach the tasty plants growing there.

Water may also help moose escape from insects. Sometimes a moose will stand with its whole body in a river or a lake. It will stick its nose out of the water so that it can breathe. Insects cannot bite a moose when it is underwater.

Being in water also helps a moose escape the extreme summer heat. That's cool!

Moose

Are All Antelope Horns the Same?

Antelope are hoofed mammals with horns. But their horns do not all look alike. Some kinds of antelope have short, straight horns. Others have long, curved horns that sometimes spiral in a twist. Some antelope horns are smooth, while others have ridges on them.

In many kinds of antelope, both males and females grow horns. But the horns of the males are usually bigger.

Antelope may look like deer, but they actually belong to the same family as goats, sheep, and cattle. Antelope horns, unlike deer antlers, grow once and last for life. Also, antelope horns never fork out in a tree-branch pattern, as do antlers. Instead, they form around a single bony core.

Antelope

What Is a Gazelle?

A gazelle is a kind of antelope. It is famous for its graceful stride—as well as for its beauty. The gazelle has large black eyes. Its horns are round and black.

The gazelle is also known for its swift movement. It can run up to 50 miles (80 kilometers) an hour. The Thomson's gazelle is one of the fastest-running mammals in all of Africa.

The gazelle is a gentle creature. The name *gazelle* comes from an Arabic word that means "to be affectionate."

Gazelle

What's Special About a Pronghorn?

The pronghorn is a hoofed mammal—an even-toed ungulate. The pronghorn is sometimes called the American antelope, but it is not really an antelope. In fact, it has no really close relatives. Scientists classify it in its own family.

The male pronghorn has horns that are 10 to 18 inches (24 to 45 centimeters) long. These horns have a bony core and a black horny covering. The pronghorn is the only animal in the world that sheds its horn covers regularly.

The pronghorn is believed to be the fastest large mammal in North America. It can run up to 60 miles (96 kilometers) an hour for short distances. It uses its speed to escape from its enemies—mainly wolves and coyotes.

Pronghorn

Who Lives on the Edge?

Mountain goats live high in the mountains. They climb on icy cliffs that might seem dangerous to us. But to a mountain goat, its home is actually safe. Not many other animals will climb that high to hunt it down.

A mountain goat's hoofs are good for safety. They are rubbery underneath, like the soles of climbing boots. The rubbery bottoms prevent the goat from slipping on the ice and rock. The goat's small hoofs give the animal a secure footing on narrow ledges.

A mountain home is a good place for these animals. Many plants and grasses grow on the high ledges. Mountain goats are one of the few kinds of animals that dare climb that high to eat the plants.

Mountain goat

How Does a Hippo Lend a Helping Hoof?

A hippo's hoof has four webbed toes. The webbing makes it easier for the hippo to walk in water. As hippos step, their hoofs stir up mud on the bottom of the lake or the river. Fish eat the creatures that the hippos dig up as they move along.

The hippo helps animals in other ways, too. It opens its mouth and lets one kind of fish eat food that is stuck in between its teeth. In return, the fish clean the hippo's skin by eating algae *(AL jee),* or tiny, plantlike bacteria, that collect on it.

Sometimes geese and other water birds help hippos, too. They sit on the hippo's back and eat insects off its skin.

Hippopotamus

What's Odd About a Rhino's Toes and Nose?

Most hoofed mammals have an even number of toes. But a rhinoceros has an odd number—three on each hoof. The middle toe is the largest. It is the main support for the rhino's heavy body. The rhino always walks on tiptoe. How odd is that!

A rhino has a fat body and short legs. You might think it couldn't run very fast. But a scared or angry rhino can run about 30 miles (48 kilometers) an hour.

A rhino's nose is also odd. The rhinoceros is the only animal with a horn on its nose. The horn may measure about 1 to 3 1/2 feet (30 to 107 centimeters) long. Some rhinos also have a second, shorter horn behind the first.

Rhinos use their horns to protect themselves against enemies. They also use them to dig up plants in the dirt to eat.

Rhinoceros

What Makes a Tapir So Unusual?

A tapir *(TAY puhr)* is a very unusual animal. It looks a lot like a pig. But it's really related to the horse, the zebra, and the rhino. But that's not the only reason a tapir is so unusual. Each of a tapir's front hoofs encases four toes—an even number. But encased in each back hoof are three toes—an odd number!

Tapirs live in tropical forests. They use their piglike snouts to sniff around for food. Tapirs eat twigs, tree leaves, shrubs, and fruit.

A tapir is a good swimmer and diver. It loves to be in water. Water is also a good place for the tapir to hide from enemies, such as tigers and leopards. The tapir can stay underwater for a long time.

Tapir

Is That a Horse with Stripes?

No, it's a zebra! But your guess is a good one, because the zebra is a member of the horse family. Like a horse, a zebra has an odd number of toes on each foot.

A zebra's entire body is covered with stripes. A zebra's stripe pattern, like a giraffe's coat pattern, is unique. No two zebras have stripes that look exactly the same.

Zebras live in the deserts and grasslands of Africa. They stay together in large herds for protection. When an enemy sees a large group of stripes, it gets confused. Zebras also have good night vision to spot danger in the dark.

Zebra

Are Hoofed Mammals in Danger?

Many hoofed mammals are in danger. Rhinos, for example, are hunted for their horns. Antelope, giraffes, and zebras are hunted for their skins, tails, or meat.

Some countries have taken action to protect hoofed mammals that are in danger. In many African countries, the hunting of endangered animals has been outlawed. There are strict fines and other penalties for poaching—hunting animals illegally.

Some hoofed mammals, such as giraffes, have lost much of their habitat to farming and cattle grazing. Governments and private organizations are now trying to save the land. They have set aside some areas as wildlife preserves. Hoofed mammals can roam freely there without the threat of farmers or hunters.

Giraffes

Hoofed Mammal Fun Facts

→ There are over 200 kinds of hoofed animals. But only 17 are odd-toed.

→ The giraffe's species is *camelopardalis,* from the Latin words for *camel* and *leopard*. A giraffe does look a bit like a spotted camel, doesn't it?

→ The tallest giraffe ever measured was 19 feet 3 inches (5.9 meters) high.

→ Less than 1 week old, a baby deer can outrun a human being.

→ A zookeeper may trim a rhino's hoofs. It's like cutting a person's fingernails.

→ A giraffe seldom uses its voice.

→ Hair on a giraffe's tail is 10 to 20 times thicker than human hair.

Glossary

acacia A thorny tree found in Africa and Australia.

adult A fully grown animal.

algae Plantlike bacteria.

antler A temporary, branch-shaped growth on the head of some hoofed mammals.

browse To eat plants and tree leaves.

calf A baby giraffe.

coat An animal's covering of fur.

cud Food that an animal partly digests and then brings back up to chew again.

dewclaws Two extra toes above each of a caribou's four hoofs.

endangered In danger of dying out.

gallop To run at the fastest speed that a hoofed mammal can go.

herbivore A mammal that eats only plants.

herd A big group of animals of one kind that stay together.

hoof The hard covering on a mammal's foot.

hoofprint The mark a hoof leaves on the ground.

horn A permanent, bonelike growth on the head of some hoofed mammals.

mammal A warm-blooded animal that feeds its young on the mother's milk.

poach To hunt animals illegally.

rock To sway from side to side.

species A group of the same kind of animals.

ungulate A hoofed mammal.

vertebrae The bones that go down the center of the back, including the seven neck bones.

waterhole A place where animals go to drink water.

webbed toes Toes that have an extra flap of skin between them.

windpipe An organ that carries air from a giraffe's mouth and nose to its lungs.

Index

(**Boldface** indicates a photo, map, or illustration.)

Picture Acknowledgments: Front & Back Cover: © Gregory G. Dimijian, Photo Researchers; © Gregory Ochocki, Photo Researchers; © Brian Miller, Bruce Coleman Inc.; © Jim Zipp, Photo Researchers.

© Mohamed Amin, Bruce Coleman Inc. 55; © Trevor Barrett, Bruce Coleman Collection 27; © Tom Brakefield, Bruce Coleman Inc. 35; © Dominique Braud, Tom Stack & Associates 39; © Nigel J. Dennis, Photo Researchers 15; © Gregory G. Dimijian, Photo Researchers 17, 61; © Jeff Foott, Tom Stack & Associates 41; © John Hyde, Bruce Coleman Inc. 37; © M.P.L. Kahl, Bruce Coleman Inc. 9; © Stephen J. Krasemann, Photo Researchers 11; © Renee Lynn, Photo Researchers 4, 59; © David Madison, Bruce Coleman Inc. 25; © Joe McDonald, Bruce Coleman Collection 5, 45, 49; © Tom McHugh, Photo Researchers 33, 57; © Brian Miller, Bruce Coleman Inc 51; © Larry Mulvehill, Photo Researchers 7; © Mark Newman, Bruce Coleman Inc. 5, 13, 21; © Gregory Ochocki, Photo Researchers 53; © Len Rue, Jr., 29, 47; © Art Wolfe, Photo Researchers 3, 23.

Illustrations: WORLD BOOK illustration by Michael DiGiorgio 6, 19, 38; WORLD BOOK illustration by Karen Donica 9.

Hoofed Mammal Classification

Scientists classify animals by placing them into groups. The animal kingdom is a group that contains all the world's animals. Phylum, class, order, and family are smaller groups. Each phylum contains many classes. A class contains orders, and a family contains individual species. Each species also has its own scientific name. Here is how the animals in this book fit in to this system.

Animals with backbones and their relatives (Phylum Chordata)

Mammals (Class Mammalia)

Even-toed ungulates (Order Artiodactyla)

Antelopes, gazelles, goats, and their relatives (Family Bovidae)

Mountain goat . . . . *Oreamnos americanus*

Deer (Family Cervidae)

Caribou (reindeer) . . . . *Rangifer terandus*
Elk . . . . *Cervus elaphus*
Moose . . . . *Alces alces*
White-tailed deer . . . . *Odocoileus virginiansus*

Giraffe and okapi (Family Giraffidae)

Giraffe . . . . *Giraffa camelopardalis*
Okapi . . . . *Okapia johnstoni*

Hippopotamuses (Family Hippopotamidae)

Pronghorn (Family Antilocapridae)

Pronghorn . . . . *Antilocapra americana*

Odd-toed ungulates (Order Perissodactyla)

Horses, zebras and their relatives (Family Equidae)

Common zebra . . . . *Equus burchelli*
Grevy's zebra . . . . *Equus grevyi*
Horse . . . . *Equus caballus*
Mountain zebra . . . . *Equus zebra*

Rhinoceroses (Family Rhinocerotidae)

Black rhinoceros . . . . *Diceros bicornis*
White rhinoceros . . . . *Ceratotherium simum*

Tapirs (Family Tapiridae)